PICASSO

A DAY IN HIS STUDIO

CONTENTS

Cover: *Portrait of Dora Maar*, 1937

Graphic design: Sandra Brys, Dominique Mazy (Zig-Zag)

First published in the United States in 1994 by
Chelsea House Publishers.

© 1993 by Casterman, Tournai

First Printing

1   3   5   7   9   8   6   4   2

ISBN 0-7910-2815-1

ART FOR CHILDREN

PICASSO
A DAY IN HIS STUDIO

By: Veronique Antoine
Translated by John Goodman

CHELSEA HOUSE PUBLISHERS
NEW YORK • PHILADELPHIA

ONE SUNDAY MORNING

 he bells of the church of Saint-Germain-des-Prés had just sounded eight o'clock.

It was the last Sunday before Christmas. I sank back into my bed and pulled the blanket up as far as my nose to warm myself. It was very cold.

My dog, Balthazar, was already at the foot of the bed, his tail wagging. His muzzle was damp and a cloud of frost emerged with his every breath. He set down his head on the edge of the mattress and, with a pleading look, made it clear he wanted me to get up for his walk. Every morning it was the same story. I jumped out of bed and threw on some pants and a sweater. I grabbed my shoes from the closet and told Balthazar I was ready. As usual, we went out onto the balcony to check out the day's temperature.

What a surprise! Snow had fallen over Paris during the night. Winter was here.

"Let's go. It's off to the river!" I took my shopping bag from the kitchen and went down the three flights. The snow had stopped falling and Seine Street, where I live, was deserted at this hour. We headed down the left sidewalk towards the baker's shop.

"Good day, Mrs. Pichon!"

"Good day, Victor, you're up bright and early this morning. Here are your bread and croissants, but be careful: they're still hot."

After leaving, Balthazar and I took Great Augustins Street. My school is on this street. My father told me its name comes from an old convent destroyed during the French revolution.

The commemorative plaque on the facade.

The front gate to Picasso's house on Great Augustins Street, as it appears today.

My eye caught something I'd never seen before—even though it's right across from school—a plaque at number seven that reads: "Pablo Picasso lived in this building from 1936 to 1955. It was in this studio that he painted *Guernica.*"

I thought to myself that Picasso must be very famous if he has this plaque on the street.

Oops! Balthazar had slipped through the gate. This was his latest trick. He liked to make me chase after him.

Balthazar was something else. He had a real knack for finding bizarre places.

**I** pushed open the cast-iron gate and entered the courtyard. It was empty, and patches of grass pushed up between the stones. Balthazar was already heading up an old spiral staircase.

What a nuisance! Stairs like this were new to him, and he was moving like a police dog on somebody's trail. He advanced with his muzzle down, sniffing for traces. What was he up to?

"Balthazar, wait! I'm coming! You'll break your legs on this twisting staircase."

The steps were worn and creaked like crazy. At certain points I stumbled, misjudging their height. The building seemed to be empty; there were spider webs everywhere.

I reached the first landing. No Balthazar. He'd kept right on climbing, of course. I could hear his steps echoing through the staircase.

"Balthazar, stop right now! Do what I say or we'll never get to the river. Are you playing police dog or something?"

There was a sign on the wall: "For Mr. Picasso, one floor higher".

That was the same name I'd just read on the plaque in the street.

This was like a game of "follow the arrows."

Fortunately, there was light from a skylight, for the stairs were getting narrower and narrower. The railing was ice cold. Finally, I arrived at the third landing. I was completely winded!

"So there you are, you old nuisance! You've completely worn me out, making me climb all these stairs."

Suddenly I saw HERE marked in giant letters next to a glazed door; it seemed to indicate a doorbell. Oddly, the door was open and I could hear a bird inside.

"Balthazar, stay with me. I'm afraid."

What was this place? Was the building really abandoned? It seemed like we should head right back down to the street.

Then I thought of Robinson Crusoe, my favorite hero. I asked myself what he would do in my place. On his desert island, he had no choice. He had to keep moving forward. Well then! Maybe you won't believe me, but that simple thought was enough to reassure me. I delicately pushed the door open. I took a few steps, and there, right in front of me, was something strange and wonderful.

A MESMERIZING
SPECTACLE

A group of figures with fixed eyes, their bodies and limbs frozen, was waiting for me. This was the first time I'd been face to face with statues bigger than I am. They seemed almost alive, and I examined their faces carefully to see if they moved or blinked. Surprisingly, I wanted to make myself small and stay there staring at them. It looked like each statue had very carefully chosen its position before adopting it forever, just like at the photographer's studio. One was pushing a baby carriage. Another held a ball. A third with a round, full-moon head held her right hand up in the air. I couldn't see all of them, for the room was dark. I'm doing my best to describe this encounter for you, but I know I'm leaving things out. Just imagine yourself in my shoes, and the surprise you'd feel! I simply can't remember everything. I'm sure that when the astronauts who landed on the moon were asked to describe their experience, they fell back on three or four vague words: unforgettable, powerful, fantastic.

A white figure was directly in front of me. His size was such that he dominated this strange assembly. I could see him very clearly. He carried a lamb in his arms. He had a gentle face and a bald head like my grandfather. He was different from the other statues, though I can't say exactly how. Suddenly—if you can believe this—he began to speak to me.

"Welcome, young man. I am called *Man with a Lamb*. Don't be afraid. I'm a talking statue, and you've just entered the studio of Pablo Picasso, one of the

The Man with a Lamb in the Great Augustins studio, 1943. This picture was taken by Brassaï, a great photographer who was a friend of Picasso. He often photographed the master's sculptures and studios. Two other works by Picasso are also visible: *The Cat* and *Female Head*.

greatest artists of this century. He lived and worked here."

"Pablo Picasso? That's the name I saw on the plaque. This is the first time I've ever heard it. What luck to have ended up in the studio of a famous man. Thanks, Balthazar!"

"All the figures you see here were painted or sculpted by him. Nothing has been moved since he left. Would you like to visit the studio?"

"Yes! I don't know anything about painting. It's a mystery to me. I like to draw at school, but the idea of doing that all your life seems strange to me."

"You may go anywhere you like, and I'll answer your questions from where I am. I'll tell you all about Picasso's life in the studio. Everything I'm going to tell you is true. Don't forget to ask your questions."

PABLO RUIZ PICASSO

Picasso went by the name Pablo Ruiz Picasso. Very early on he started to use his mother's family name, Picasso, because he thought it was more interesting than Ruiz. And what's your name?"

"Victor. Where should I begin?"

"You should get to know Picasso's face first of all. There's a photograph on the table. Have a look."

"What eyes! They look like they could swallow you up!"

"Sit down in this armchair. I'll tell you his life story. Picasso was born in Malaga, Spain, in 1881. At his birth, the midwife thought he'd been born dead. Fortunately, his doctor, who was also his uncle, was there to save him. His father, Don José Ruiz, was a painter.

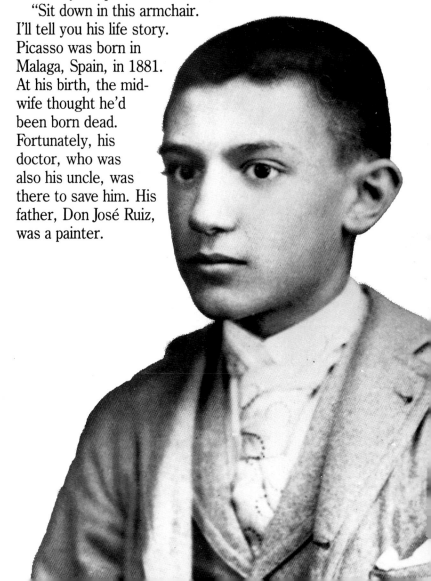

Picasso in 1896. He had just arrived in Barcelona, where his father had assumed a position at the school of fine arts.

The house in Malaga in which Picasso was born.

"Picasso didn't like school. He preferred to take drawing class. One day, his father asked him to complete one of his paintings. The result so impressed Pablo's father that he decided to lay down his own brushes for good, saying that he was abandoning painting because his son was already more accomplished than he was."

"This is the first time I've heard a story about a son who was more accomplished than his father! My father always knows what's best for me. It gets annoying sometimes.

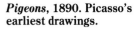

Pigeons, 1890. Picasso's earliest drawings.

"Why did Picasso come to Paris?"

"At the time, it was a great artistic center full of painters, poets, and musicians. Picasso settled here at age 20. He was poor and alone. All the canvases he painted were blue. This color seemed to correspond to his state of mind then. He saw all of life as blue."

"But blue isn't really a sad color."

"No, it is cold and deep. These years are now called his 'blue period.' "

"Did he live here?"

"No. Picasso first settled in Montmartre, where there were many Spanish people. He moved into a studio in the Bateau-Lavoir, which in French means laundry boat."

"What an odd name. Was it a really a boat?"

Life, better known by its French title, *La Vie*, 1903.

Self Portrait, 1901. Picasso was 20 at the time.

The Laundry Boat. Photo by Brassaï.

"Not at all. It was a big house in Montmartre where lots of artists lived. With its hallways and twisting stairs it resembled a boat. It was dirty, and there was no electricity or running water. In winter the water froze and in summer it was unbearably hot. But Picasso remained there for nine years.

"It was there that he painted *Les Demoiselles d'Avignon* (*The Young Girls of Avignon*), a painting that shocked all his friends and revolutionized painting. No previous painting had contained such grotesque faces and violently deformed bodies."

"Was it a blue painting?"

"No, the blue period was over. In the meantime, Picasso had fallen in love with a young woman named Fernande. He had also discovered the world of the circus by attending the Medrano Circus. He was delighted by its acrobats, jugglers, clowns, and harlequin figures. He painted lots of harlequins. With this new life, he adopted new colors: rose and ochre. This was his rose period. *Les Demoiselles d'Avignon* was painted in these colors."

"Were there a lot of different periods?"

Family of Acrobats with an Ape, 1905.

"Yes! All of his work was linked to his life. He painted the way you would keep a diary. Each period corresponded to an important change in his existence. He said, 'Whenever I've had something to say, I've said it in the way that seemed best to me.'"

Les Demoiselles d'Avignon (The Young Girls of Avignon), **1907. In this painting Picasso broke violently with tradition. For the first time, a painter disregarded considerations of resemblance. By so doing, he opened the way to modern art.**

"My goodness! It sounds like your story is going to be long. I'd better make myself comfortable. Can I eat my croissant?"

"Yes, go right ahead. My story is long because Picasso never stopped inventing. His painting *Les Demoiselles d'Avignon* opened the following period, that of cubism, during which Picasso and his friend Georges Braque found a new way to paint things: from the front and sides all at once."

"Why was it called cubism?"

"That's simple. It comes from the word 'cube.' Picasso and Braque reduced forms to geometric shapes and cubes. Then they painted the objects from all sides at once. They also invented collage."

"Was Picasso famous?"

"As a matter of fact, it was cubism that made him famous. But he didn't stop there. Afterwards, a friend asked him to do the sets for a ballet in Rome. He got to know a Russian member of the dance troupe named Olga Koklova. Soon they were married. Under her influence Picasso began to lead a more glittering social life. They took seaside vacations, and Picasso began to paint bathers. They look like statues. Don't forget that in Rome he'd just seen lots of ancient statues."

"And Fernande?"

"She'd been long since forgotten. Picasso loved many women in his long life. They were named Fernande, Eva, Olga, Marie-Thérèse, Dora, Françoise, and Jacqueline. All of them inspired him and can be seen in many of his works. He got married twice and had four children."

"So what did he do next?"

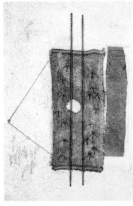

In 1926, Picasso conceived this *Guitar*, a work made from objects intended for other purposes: burlap, string, nails, and a strip of newspaper. At this time he frequently saw many surrealist poets such as André Breton, Philippe Soupault, and Pierre Reverdy.

"Suddenly there was a new violence in his work. His mood had changed. Look at this collage representing a guitar that's made with nails—nails that are pointing out! Picasso agreed with this saying by André Breton: 'Beauty must be convulsive or it is nothing.' "

"What does 'convulsive' mean?"

"Agitated, violent. Picasso subjected the human face and body to monstrous deformations. The colors became aggressive. People didn't like these paintings."

Two Women Running on the Beach, 1922.
A study for the curtain for the ballet *Le Train Bleu*, with a scenario by Jean Cocteau and music by Darius Milhaud.

"So when did he move here?"

"After he broke with Olga. At first it was just his studio. When war broke out, he moved in completely. This was his sculpture studio. His painting studio, bedroom, and bathroom are upstairs."

"Did Picasso fight in the war?"

"No. He lived through several wars, but as a foreigner, and he never enlisted in the army. Painting and sculpture were his instruments of war.

"In an immense painting in black and

white called *Guernica*, he denounced the inhumanity of the Spanish Civil War. He painted it in these very rooms, after having read a brief but terrible newspaper report: 'Yesterday the historic Basque village of Guernica was completely destroyed by bombing.' The bombers attacked on April 26, 1937.

"Picasso never went back to his native country."

Guernica, 1937. Picasso made 45 preparatory studies for this painting in black, white, and gray, which is quite large (11 feet 6 inches × 25 feet 8 inches, or 349.3 × 776.6 cm.). It is a scream of protest against the massacre of defenseless civilians by Nazi bombers. As a result of this atrocity, 1,654 people died and 889 were wounded. Most of the victims were women and children.

"Did Picasso like living here?"

"Yes, very much. He chose this place because it appealed to him. Artists' studios are important places for them. They need to feel comfortable there. Entering an artist's studio is a bit like uncovering a secret. Picasso referred to his studio as a laboratory."

"If he liked it so much, why did he leave?"

"Picasso was a man of the south. He always loved the sun and the heat. He and Olga had already vacationed on the southern coast of France. At the time, it wasn't swarming with tourists as it is now. He returned to the region regularly, and one day he decided to settle there for good."

"My grandfather lives in Nice. Can I see Picasso's house the next time I pay him a visit?"

"Picasso lived in several houses in the south: in Antibes, Vallauris, Cannes, Vauvenargues, and Mougins. But you can't visit them. It was in Vallauris that he discovered ceramics. He quickly developed a passion for this medium, producing works of great audacity. He made pitchers shaped like animals and vases shaped like heads. Such was the nature of Picasso's genius. He managed to transform every material he touched. A real magician!"

"That's like Leonardo da Vinci, who could do just about everything: not only painting and building, but mathematics, hydraulics, and

Bullfighting motif from a plate.

Plate decorated with a bull's head.

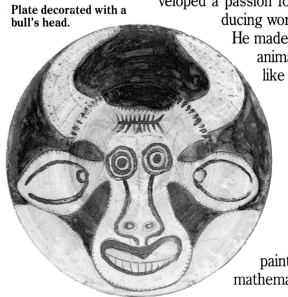

Bull Goring a Horse, 1934. This large canvas (97 × 130 cm, or about 38 × 51 feet) has an impressive power. The horse with its head straining heavenward, gored by a bull, already announces *Guernica*. In Picasso's work, these two animals often symbolize, respectively, good and evil.

engineering as well. Why didn't Picasso ever go back to Spain?"

"Because he opposed the Franco government there. But he remained deeply connected to his country. To take one example, he loved bullfighting and made lots of images with matadors and bulls."

"Olé! Olé! Look out, Balthazar, or I'll get up and charge you!"

Picasso and his friend, the writer Jean Cocteau, trying on bullfighters' hats and capes in Vallauris.

"I forgot to mention the sculpture-assemblages. The best known one is the head of a bull. Picasso made it with the handlebars and seat of a bicycle he found on the street."

"Fantastic! I really like that one. I also keep my eye out for interesting odds and ends when I'm walking with Balthazar. I keep them in a closed cabinet, and always carry the key."

"The two of you would have understood one another. Picasso brought back to the studio all sorts of things he'd found in garbage cans. He once said: 'I only like objects without value, rubbish.'

Head of a Bull, 1943.
Sculpture-assemblage.

"His friend Cocteau nicknamed him 'the king of the rag pickers.' Picasso combined objects in unexpected ways to create assemblages. Then he turned them into sculptures."

"How did he die?"

"Toward the end of his life, when he was world famous, Picasso lived a very retired life with his new wife Jacqueline. They were married when Picasso was 80 years old. He continued to work with intense energy until the eve of his death."

Woman with Baby Carriage, 1950. Bronze, cast after an assemblage including pottery vases and handles, plates of sheet iron, a stovepipe, a colander with its bottom cut away, and a child's cart.

an with a Lamb, can I sit down at this table with pen and paper? I want to describe the studio and then copy what I've written into my diary."

"Do whatever you like."

I arrived in a small entryway full of plants where there was also a cage with two birds inside. Question: How can they survive here? Then I passed into an oblong room. Disorder was everywhere. Guitars, hats, enormous piles of mail, cigarette packs, photographs, newspapers, and books covered all the furniture. Only two black armchairs were empty. The floor was covered with matting. There were frames, paintings, and boxes of drawings all over the place. I laughed when I saw an armchair covered in worn velvet with a painted face sitting on it and slippers at its feet. Further on was the big room with statues. Near the door was a ladder with two paintings leaning against it.

Picasso, *Still Life with Lemons and Oranges.* A subject close to that in Matisse's painting on the opposite page, but handled very differently. Here everything is in conflict.

"The oranges in this painting are superb!"

"They were painted by Henri Matisse. He was the painter Picasso admired the most. He like to be surrounded by his painting collection when he worked."

Matisse's *"Still Life with Oranges"* in the Great Augustins Studio, 1943. Photo by Brassai. Also visible, at right, is *Montsouris Park* by Douanier Rousseau. Picasso had great admiration for both these artists.

"What disorder! Finding something in here would be like looking for a needle in a haystack."

"Picasso knew exactly where everything was. If something was moved without his knowledge he would become very angry. One day his friend Brassaï moved Picasso's slippers to take a photo, and Picasso noticed it immediately."

"And who did the housecleaning?"

"A maid named Inès. Poor creature! Picasso forbade anyone to clean his studio. He thought the dust provided an excellent protective covering."

"You know, I like it here. I feel as though Picasso will be coming home tonight. Probably because of the mess and the birds."

I had finished writing. I folded the page and slipped it into my pocket so I wouldn't forget it. But now I wanted to have a closer look at the statues.

Chair with Slippers in the Great Augustins Studio. Photo by Brassaï.

Matisse, *Still life with Oranges*, 1913. Here all is color and harmony.

27

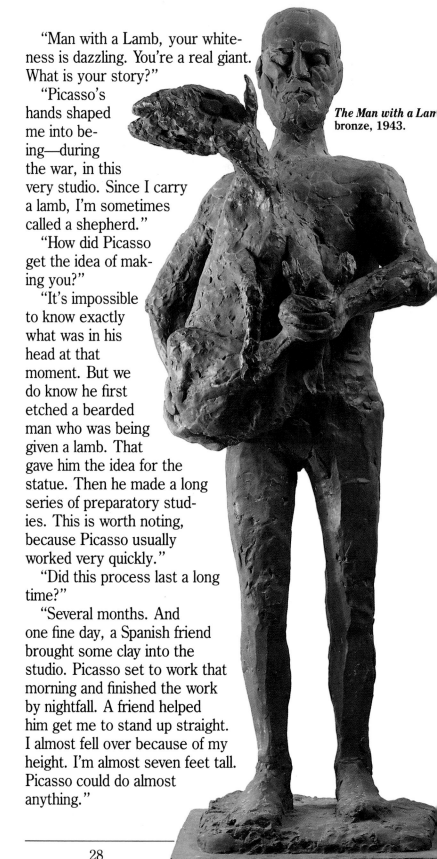

"Man with a Lamb, your white-ness is dazzling. You're a real giant. What is your story?"

"Picasso's hands shaped me into be-ing—during the war, in this very studio. Since I carry a lamb, I'm sometimes called a shepherd."

"How did Picasso get the idea of mak-ing you?"

"It's impossible to know exactly what was in his head at that moment. But we do know he first etched a bearded man who was being given a lamb. That gave him the idea for the statue. Then he made a long series of preparatory stud-ies. This is worth noting, because Picasso usually worked very quickly."

"Did this process last a long time?"

"Several months. And one fine day, a Spanish friend brought some clay into the studio. Picasso set to work that morning and finished the work by nightfall. A friend helped him get me to stand up straight. I almost fell over because of my height. I'm almost seven feet tall. Picasso could do almost anything."

The Man with a Lamb
bronze, 1943.

"And he painted you white?"

"No, I'm white because I'm a plaster cast of the clay original. He also cast me in bronze."

"You know, your bald head makes you look a bit like my grandfather from Nice. That's why I liked you from the start."

"My face is probably the most human one in all of Picasso's sculpture. At the same time he made me, he was painting faces ravaged by pain because of the war. Perhaps he saw me as an image of peace and reconciliation."

"Man with a Lamb, I'm going to write a whole page about you in my diary!"

Woman Crying, 1937.

29

Getting to the other end of the studio wasn't easy. It was like crossing an obstacle course! I had to climb over or around statues and objects of every conceivable kind. A small room, invisible from the entryway, was hidden at the back. Near its entrance was the statue of a woman who looked forbidding. Her left arm was raised in the air and seemed to say: "Stop!" I say she was a woman because she wore a kind of pleated skirt, but in reality I don't know what universe she came from. She carried a branch of foliage. I couldn't tell how old she was. Her square head, with holes bored in it, made me think of a Martian, but her upraised arm made me think of an ancient statue.

"You know, Mrs. Statue, if I stop in front of you, it's not because I'm afraid of you. Not at all. Whether you're a goddess or a Martian, you intrigue me.

"Perhaps you keep watch over a treasure and don't want me to enter this room. I know how to find out.

"Man with a Lamb, what is the story behind this statue?"

"She's called *Woman with Foliage* and was born entirely of Picasso's imagination. She doesn't have any other story. She was made in 1934, at the moment Picasso started to experiment with imprints of objects in plaster."

"Oh, I've done that at school. It's easy. You take a hard object and you push it into fresh plaster. First I did it with some tree bark, but then I made an imprint with my own hand."

"Picasso did the same thing with his.

For *Woman with Foliage*, he took the top of a box, drilled some holes in it, and made a plaster cast of it. Presto! He had a face with two eyes and a mouth. But you can see that much for yourself."

"Yes, even though it's rectangular, I understood immediately that it's a face."

"Exactly. When you look at this sculpture, you immediately see a nose, a mouth, two eyes, and a long dress. Picasso said, 'What you have to do is name things. Things must be called by their names. That's all that's required.'

"If things get called by their right names, then that's enough."

"In other words, two holes equals two eyes, and a line equals a mouth. It's easy to paint like that; it's the bare minimum."

"You've just used a word that's very important for modern art: minimum. Earlier on, painters tried to create resemblance by using a maximum of details. Modern art took the opposite course: simplification."

"That's easier."

"I don't think so."

"Why is the head rectangular? It's not like that in reality!"

"Precisely. It's meant to surprise you. This sculpture belongs to the universe of art, where heads can be rectangular. In art nothing is prohibited."

"Is it real foliage?"

"Yes, a cast of it. She holds it like a ghost. Perhaps he was thinking of a princess or a goddess when he made her."

"So I was right. She's wearing a dress."

"Yes. It looks like the tunic of a Greek goddess, but Picasso used corrugated cardboard to make it. He was some magician!"

"Abracadabra. Ladies and gentlemen, I give you Picasso, the greatest magician in the world. He can make sculptures out of anything, anything at all!"

"His wife Jacqueline once said, 'You can't leave even a bit of thread lying about without him making something from it.' "

"And finally, does this Woman with Foliage guard a treasure?"

"In a sense. She keeps watch over a room that Picasso kept secret. He alone had the key to it."

"Can I go in?"

"Yes."

THE SHOWCASE

I passed the statue, with its mocking air, and entered the tiny room. On one side there was a showcase and on the other a bench and tools that made me think of a carpenter's studio.

I pressed my nose up against the glass door of the showcase. There was so much to see! Five shelves that were absolutely crammed.

Suddenly I thought of my own room with its locked cabinet full of treasures. It paled beside Picasso's, even with the two parrot feathers I'd collected a few days ago. This disappointed me, for I was very fond of it. But I took consolation in the fact that both of us clearly liked boxes and rocks. In any case, comparison was pointless. He was older than me and, what's more, he had traveled. So it was only normal that he would have more treasures than I did.

I took the pen and paper out of my pocket and wrote down what I saw. I won't deny that I intended to steal some of his ideas for my own collection. There were statuettes, pebbles, bones, skeletons, painted boxes, packing boxes, a pair of gloves, a relief covered with sand, masks, plates, and a little wooden horse.

"Is the showcase locked?"

"Not literally. Picasso said it was his museum. He only allowed close friends to see it. He arranged souvenirs, fetish objects of which he was particularly fond, and works of his own in it."

"I have the impression he loved ancient things, like all these statuettes. Some are as thin as knife blades."

"Yes, he was deeply interested in antiquities from the entire world.

"In this period, many artists became fascinated by African, Oceanic, and Asian art. Artists like Paul Gauguin, Henri Matisse, Amedeo Modigliani, and Picasso found inspiration in these artifacts."

"But didn't people know about them earlier?"

"No, this was a revelation for the Western artists of our century. Modern art was born of this encounter."

"And Picasso was involved?"

"He was one of the leaders in this development. Cubism was partly inspired by Spanish primitive art and African masks."

"So he didn't invent anything new. He just copied the work of others."

"Not exactly, for the secret of his power was that he could transform anything. For example: an African mask became the face of one of the *Demoiselles d'Avignon*, in the painting I've already told you about. Picasso transformed these objects into something that was his."

"He was a clever fellow. You know, I'm almost jealous of his showcase. I wish I could have met this Picasso."

Picasso owned a collection of primitive art. This statue of a woman from New Caledonia figured in it. Picasso discovered African and Oceanic art in 1907, on a visit to the Museum of Man at the Trocadéro in Paris.

Figurines in Sculpted Wood, 1932. Picasso carved these statuettes with a knife. He deliberately left them in this rough state, as he wanted to preserve the original structure of the wood.

THE WOMAN IN A LONG DRESS

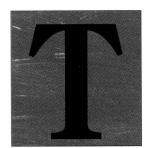

T hen I continued my little tour.

I discovered a curious statue. She was wearing a real painter's smock.

I approached her. She had a wooden body and a head made of clay.

"Picasso cheated with this one! He used a real palette, real brushes, and a real smock to dress this statue. That's too easy. It isn't sculpture; it's just games."

"At first she was called *Woman in a Long Dress*. Picasso had run across an old wooden mannequin from the turn of the century. He bought it and modeled a head and one arm for it. Then he attached another wooden arm from Easter Island given him by a friend."

"And the painter's paraphernalia?"

"Picasso loved to dress up, just like children do. One day, for a photograph, he amused himself by adding things he had lying around the studio, including a glass palette that he'd received from the United States. He set the statue in front of a painting, and she became *Woman with a Palette*."

"That's just puttering about. I could do it myself. In fact, why don't I dress up a mannequin and then I'll be an artist. What do think, Balthazar? I'll have a huge studio and you'll be able to do whatever you like in it. No more school, no more math, no more taking notes. Tempting, isn't it?

"This lady is funny: I don't know why, but with her hair in a bun she made me think of old governesses in the movies."

"The simpler works of art seem, the more we think we could do as well. Let me ask you this: the last time you saw a

Woman in a Long Dress.
The statue as it appears today.

Woman with a Palette.
Photo by Brassaï, 1946.
This work existed only
for the photograph, at
least as it is seen here
with smock and palette.
Picasso enjoyed
arranging such short-
lived tableaux.

mannequin in a shop, did you think about
transforming it like this?"

"When I see a mannequin, I see a
mannequin and that's all. I don't think
about anything else."

"Exactly! But it wasn't like that with
Picasso. When he saw something or got
hold of it, he transformed it in his imagination. In Picasso's hands, this mannequin became a haunting statue."

"The next time I see a mannequin, I'll
think about this Woman with a Palette."

"And you'll be reminded of Picasso."

AND IF I WERE PICASSO?

Suddenly an idea came to me. What if I pretended to be Picasso at work in his studio?

I began by tying back my hair in a ponytail. I opened my eyes very wide like in the photographs. I pulled up the sleeves of my shirt and jacket.

It was cold! An artist's life is hard.

I imagined that it was morning, and that he'd finished dressing and had his breakfast. Now it was time to read the mail.

I settled into a wicker rocking chair. I took a pile of mail from the table and examined the stamps. I thought about my buddy Joey, who collects stamps. He'd be wild with jealousy if he could see them!

Oh! An envelope from America. Let's see what's inside. It's a letter from an art dealer named Kahnweiler. Not very interesting.

"He must have spent a lot of time answering his mail."

"Picasso almost never answered letters. It would have taken up too much of his time. He used to hang important correspondence on wires with clothespins so he wouldn't forget about it."

"That must have made for a funny kind of decoration! When I talk to you does my voice resemble Picasso's?"

"Not at all. Picasso always retained a strong Spanish accent, and there was always a hint of song in his voice."

"Oh! That's hard to imitate. Sort of like people from the south of France?"

"Sort of."

Picasso in front of the *Portrait of Yadwigha* by Douanier Rousseau. Photo by Brassaï, 1932.

I tried out an accent with more sing-song in it.

"Is that better?"

"Yes, that's a bit closer."

If I spoke with an accent all the time, in the end I wouldn't be able to talk any other way, and my parents would be surprised when I got home. I guess I could always tell them I was speaking like Picasso.

"Did he read his mail in this chair?"

"No, never."

"I'm beginning to think it's impossible to pretend to be Picasso. Let's end this game. I've never met an artist, and I don't know how they live."

"Don't get angry. I'll talk you through one of his days, and that way you'll have a better idea. How about it?"

"All right, but I want to change chairs; this rocking is making me dizzy. I'll stretch out on the matting and close my eyes. While you tell me about things, I'll try to imagine them. We do that all the time in my theater class."

At the end of his life Picasso had another photographer friend, Edward Quinn, who took many photos of the artist's daily life.

icasso's days always unfolded pretty much the same way.

"When Picasso woke up, Inès, his maid, came into his bedroom with his breakfast. He usually had coffee with milk and two biscuits."

"Can you describe Inès to me? That will make it easier for me to imagine the scene."

"She was a young, black-haired woman with a sunny disposition and golden skin. She often wore flower-print dresses."

"Was her room as messy as this one?"

"Things were crowded in her quarters, too. Picasso slept in a big copper bed under a blanket of cow fur with white spots. The rest of the furniture consisted of a chest of drawers, a desk, and a chair. The only other ornament was a wood-burning heater in the middle of the room."

"Did he get up late?"

"That varied. After Inès, Sabartès came in with the day's mail and newspapers. Sabartès was Picasso's faithful friend, confidant, and secretary. He took care of correspondence, received visitors, and helped prepare exhibitions. He wore thick glasses and had a rather sad face."

"Did he work here, in this room?"

"Exactly."

"During breakfast Picasso glanced at his mail. He had a hard time getting the day started and was often in a bad mood in the morning. Fortunately, he had his companion Françoise to make things a bit easier. She was also part of his closest circle."

"He didn't work in the morning?"

"No. Until about 1:00 P.M., he received visitors either here or upstairs. It was a parade of friends, curiosity seekers, and art dealers. There were a few who came most every day, mainly poets and writers."

"So the mornings were quite gay, then."

"Not always. Picasso had serious discussions with his guests. He showed them his latest paintings because he needed to observe their reactions in order to continue his work. At one o'clock the house emptied and Picasso went down to have lunch with his friends at the Catalan, his favorite restaurant."

"Can I see it from the window?"

"Once you could have, because it was right on Great Augustins Street, but now it's gone."

"I think I could get to like a morning schedule like that. Breakfast in bed, conversation with friends, and then lunch at a restaurant. The life of a king!"

"Yes, but now you must hear about the second part of his day. After lunch Picasso thought of only one thing: work. He went into his studio and remained alone there, painting or sculpting. Visits and telephone calls were not allowed to interrupt him. He stopped long enough to have dinner in the small kitchen and then continued working late into the night. When the light faded, he shined two projectors directly onto the painting he was completing. In his own words, 'There must be complete darkness around the canvas if the painter is to be hypnotized by his work.' "

"It's a shame I haven't yet seen the upstairs studio where he painted. But if I had to choose, I think I'd prefer to be Picasso in the morning."

"If you only focus on that part of his life you're forgetting what was most important about it. Picasso always gave his work first priority."

"He never wanted to stop painting?"

"There was a period of several months in his life when he couldn't paint. So he started to write, and one day he was ready to paint again. You need to eat to live. Picasso had to eat, too, but he also needed to work."

"I don't know anything about this work bug, and I suspect I'll never catch it. Now that you've told me about Picasso's day, I see that it's impossible to pretend to be Picasso without having met him. He was too different from everyone else. I don't know anyone like him. Didn't he ever get tired?"

"Some say he never did. He himself said, 'I was in a hurry every night to get back to work. I wanted to see what would happen.' "

"Now that I know all about his schedule, I think it's time to go upstairs.

"Gosh, look at all the dust on my pants from the matting. I'll brush it off later.

"Come on, Balthazar, we're going up to the other studio. Do we take the stairs at the back of the big room?"

"Yes."

Picasso at work on a view of his studio in Vallauris. Photo by E. Quinn. Picasso continued to work energetically until the very end of his life.

THE PAINTING STUDIO

Work table in the Great Augustins studio, 1945. Photo by Brassaï.

e headed up the wooden stairs. They creaked at the slightest pressure. It was dangerous because I couldn't see very much.

One more step and then—oops!

"Oh! Terrific! I'd love to have a room like this." It was like an attic; there were roof-beams and dormer-windows, and the walls were slanted.

Fortunately, there were thick beams holding them up.

"Man with a Lamb, can you hear me?"

"You don't need to yell. I can hear you very well."

"Can I open one of the windows? I'm afraid of suffocating from this painting smell."

"You're too short to reach the windows."

Suddenly Balthazar started to cough. He was allergic to these odors.

"Poor Balthazar, get away from there. You just parked yourself under the one table up here that's covered with paints.

"Did this table serve as Picasso's palette?"

"That's right. Picasso didn't use a real palette. He mixed his paints directly on the table, which he covered with a thick layer of newspaper. When they got too messy he just changed them."

"This Picasso never did anything like everyone else!"

It was fantastic to see all these painting instruments. The empty frames everywhere made it feel like an artist's materials shop. I'd be afraid to paint canvases that were so big.

But I'd come to understand that this disorder was typical of Picasso.

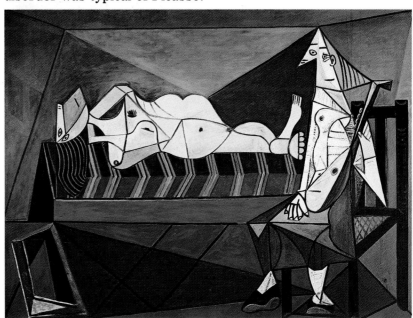

Dawn Song, 1942.

KASBEK'S RUG

I was startled. Balthazar had taken hold of the end of a rug with his teeth and started to growl. He loves to do this at home with my clothes or the rags in his basket. It always makes me laugh. But we weren't at home.

"Balthazar, stop right now! You'll damage the rug. You're crazy!"

No question, he's as stubborn as a mule. He was going to tear the rug to pieces unless I did something. But I was too late. Balthazar slid under a piece of furniture with the rug. He was safe there; I couldn't reach him.

I was getting more and more annoyed. What should I do? I had an idea. I pretended I was leaving the room. I headed toward the stairs.

But the Man with a Lamb spoke to me: "Leave your dog alone. Balthazar smells Kasbek, Picasso's dog. Kasbek often slept on that rug."

"Picasso's dog lived here?"

"Yes, and he was treated like a king. He was the only visitor who had access to Picasso when he worked. One day Picasso even said, 'Since I work with Kasbek, I make paintings that bite.'"

"I've never heard of anyone being bitten by a painting."

"He was speaking figuratively. Picasso meant to say that his paintings were surprising and left strong impressions in the minds of those who saw them."

"What kind of dog was he?"

"An Afghan greyhound with shaggy hair only around his ears. This breed was little known in France. When Marcel the chauffeur took Kasbek for walks, every-

The Dog Kasbek in the Great Augustins Studio. Photo by Brassaï, 1944.

body asked him about the dog. So one day Picasso said to him, 'Marcel, when people ask you about the breed of my dog, tell them it's a lunatic basset hound, they'll be so taken aback that they'll leave you alone.' "

"Were there any other animals, besides Kasbek?"

"There were some turtledoves and canaries that lived in the entryway and the kitchen. For a while, he kept an owl that he'd brought back from Antibes. Once, he even brought home a monkey, but he had to get rid of it. He painted lots of pigeons, like his father. To illustrate a poster for a peace conference, he chose a dove. This image has become world famous. He even called his daughter Paloma, which means 'dove.' "

During this conversation, Balthazar had abandoned his prize. I calmly picked it up and put it back where it had been.

Dove poster.

AN ODD EXHIBITION

here was an odd arrangement of things near the window that I hadn't noticed—paintings stacked against one another and posed against an easel. They were precariously balanced. Finally, there was an exhibition my own height. Usually, I hated going to museums with my parents because everything was too high for me to see.

"Balthazar, come lie down on this bench. You can be my cushion."

We always did that on the couch at home. I stretched out and took a long look. It was terrific.

"Tell me, Man with a Lamb, was this exhibition designed especially for me?"

"If you like. Picasso very often arranged his works like this for visitors. He loved these improvised presentations. All the faces you see really existed. I'll introduce you to them in the proper order, beginning at the upper left. That's Ambroise Vollard, the picture dealer. He organized Picasso's first exhibition in Paris in 1901. It wasn't a great success. Over there is Olga Kokhlova, Picasso's first wife. And Paulo, their son, dressed up as a harlequin. And here's Marie-Thérèse Walter. Picasso met her while strolling alongside the Lafayette Galleries in Paris. He introduced himself by saying, 'Miss, you have a very interesting face. I would like to do your portrait. I am Picasso.'

"Here is Maya, his first daughter. Finally, there's Françoise Gilot as a woman-flower. She lived here in the studio."

"I can't quite believe that these are the portraits of real people."

aul as Pierrot, 1925.

"Picasso once said, 'My friends and those I love are the source of my inspiration.' Don't forget that Picasso wasn't a photographer; he was a painter. In his portraits, he represented not only what he saw, but also what he thought and felt about the person. And yet the subjects always remain recognizable. Picasso said, 'When I paint, I always try to come up with an image that's unexpected.' "

had a hard time believing that Picasso had painted all these portraits. They were so different from one another.

"Do you draw now the same way you did when you were younger?"

"No, my drawing has changed a lot."

"The same with Picasso. He didn't want to paint the same way all his life. In his portraits, he changed his way of painting in response to the appearance, character, and feelings of his model."

"The one I like best in the series is Olga, because the likeness seems most convincing. The one of the picture dealer is awful. I can't make any sense of it."

"Why should we always want to understand things? Picasso once said, 'We never try to understand the song of a bird. We never ask ourselves why we love the night, or a flower. But everyone wants to understand painting.' Here, since the figure and the background blend together, the picture is difficult to read."

"Is this one of the cubist portraits you mentioned?"

"Yes, exactly. The portrait itself almost disappears. Only the mouth, eyes, eyebrows, and nose can easily be made out. The use of the yellow-ochre color helps a bit; it shows us the limits of the face. But despite the clash of shattered forms, the portrait resembles Vollard."

"This Mr. Vollard must have been a real kaleidoscope. Are you sure it resembles him?"

"Yes. Vollard told how the four-year-old daughter of one of his friends said immediately on seeing this portrait, 'It's Vollard.'"

Woman-Flower, 1946.

Portrait of Ambroise Vollard, 1910.

"The strangest one is this flower portrait. It must be completely imaginary."

"Not at all. It's Françoise Gilot. Matisse had said something about painting Françoise with green hair. Picasso picked up on this idea and made her hair into leaves."

"Madame Gilot must have burst out laughing when she saw this portrait."

"I wouldn't be so sure. Picasso was very happy with this painting, and made the following remark to her about it: 'We all resemble animals of some kind, but not you. You have the energy of a spring plant. I don't know what made me represent you in this way. It's bizarre, but it's definitely you.' "

THE TWO WOMEN IN ARMCHAIRS

althazar was beginning to fidget. The bench wasn't comfortable for him.

"Get down, dog. I'll do without you. Do what you like, but I'm still not finished with my exhibition. There are still these two women in armchairs who are giving me strange looks. Were their eyes really like that? I can't tell where they're looking."

"This is cubism again. Take a good look at the blue face. The nose and mouth are in profile, but the two eyes and a blue area suggesting another nose are seen from the front. In this portrait, we see Marie-Thérèse Walter from the front and the side at the same time."

"Why yes, you're right."

"Now try to guess something about the character of these two women in their chairs."

"That's hard. I'd say the one wearing a hat seems gentle and dreamy. The other one, with her pointed nose and fingers, is much more forbidding. I prefer the first one."

"They had very different characters which Picasso expressed in line and color. The first one, with its curved, flowing lines and soft, cool colors like green and blue, is Marie-Thérèse Walter, the dreamer. The second one has pointed lines and shrill colors. She is Dora Maar, who was intelligent and authoritarian. Picasso managed to capture each of their personalities using shapes and colors that were appropriate to them."

"I think this face in lemon yellow and green is horrible. She looks like she's wearing clown makeup."

*Portrait of Marie-Thérèse
Walter*, 1937.

Portrait of Dora Maar, 1937.

"At the beginning of this century, painting stopped being a simple reproduction of the world. Color was liberated. A tree could be blue, or an eye green. Do you understand?"

"A bit better, I suppose. Is that the chair from the vestibule?"

"Exactly. Picasso mostly painted his circle and the things around him. This chair was in the studio, so he put it in the painting. Picasso never painted things that were entirely imaginary, he always started with reality."

There was complete silence in the studio. I was tired of talking; that was enough for today. I had heard so many stories! It would take me days and days to write them all down in my diary. But I wasn't afraid; I could start during Christmas vacation.

The bells at the church of Saint-Germain-des-Prés rang 12 times.

I could make it back home just in time for lunch. My parents would probably think that Balthazar and I just took a long walk like we do every Sunday. Should I tell them about this adventure in Picasso's house? If I say I've been talking with a statue, they'll think I've made the story up and will make fun of me. I prefer to keep it a secret between Balthazar and me, especially since the Man with the Lamb told me that experiences like this don't happen twice.

Summary Chronology

1881	Pablo Ruiz Picasso is born in Malaga, Spain on October 25; his father, Don José Ruiz, is a drawing teacher.
1892	Enters school of fine arts in La Corogne.
1895	The family settles in Barcelona; first large canvas, *First Communion*.
1895	Enters Royal Academy of San Fernando in Madrid.
1899	Returns to Barcelona; meets his future secretary, Jaime Sabartès, and Casagemas.
1900	First sojourn in Paris with Casagemas; returns to Barcelona in December.
1901	Second Paris sojourn; first Parisian exhibition at Vollard's gallery; meets the poet Max Jacob; *Self-Portrait in Blue*.
1904	Settles permanently in Paris in Le Bateau Lavoir; meets the poet Guillaume Apollinaire.
1905	Fernande Olivier becomes his companion; exhibits his first rose-period paintings.
1906	Meets Henri Matisse; spends the summer in Gosol, Spain.
1907	*Les Demoiselles d'Avignon*; meets Georges Braque.
1908	Braque's first cubist exhibition.
1912	A new companion, Marcelle Humbert (Eva); first collages; *Still Life with Chair Caning*.
1915	Death of Eva; meets Jean Cocteau.
1917	Sojourn in Rome to execute sets and costumes for the ballet *Parade*; meets the dancer Olga Koklova.
1918	Marries Olga; moves to Boétie Street in Paris.
1919	Vacations in Saint-Raphaël; first Mediterranean canvases.
1921	Birth of his son Paul.
1922	Prepares sets for Cocteau's *Antigone*; summers in Dinard.
1924–25	Paints a series of large still lifes.
1925	*The Dance*; takes part in the first surrealist exhibition.
1926	Paints a series of *Guitars*.
1927	Meets Marie-Thérèse Walter.
1928	Collaborates on a series of iron sculptures with Julio González.
1931	Settles in the Boisgeloup chateau.
1932	Marie-Thérèse Walter becomes his companion; prepares a series of sculpted heads of Marie-Thérèse.
1934	Travels in Spain with Olga and Paul; prepares a series of molded sculptures.
1935	Breaks with Olga; birth of Maya, the daughter of Picasso and Marie-Thérèse Walter.
1936	Meets Dora Maar.
1937	Picasso takes a studio at no. 7, Great Augustins Street; paints *Guernica*.
1938–39	Paints a series of portraits of women; lives in Royan for a year.
1941	Writes a play, *Desire Caught by the Tail*.
1943	Meets Françoise Gilot; completes *Man with a Lamb*.
1945	Joins the Communist Party.
1945	Françoise Gilot becomes his companion; first lithographs.
1946	Lives and works at the museum in Antibes.
1947	Makes first ceramics in Vallauris; birth of Claude.
1948	Moves to Vallauris.

PICASSO'S PERIODS

There is an infinite formal variety in the whole of Picasso's work. Colors, shapes, materials, and themes change and evolve ceaselessly. These continuing metamorphoses are sometimes difficult to follow and understand. For convenience, certain works have come to be grouped together by period. Here is a brief account of the most important ones.

Blue Period: 1901–1904
"I started painting in blue while I was thinking about Casagemas' death." Casagemas, a faithful friend, committed suicide in 1901 in the wake of a failed love affair. For three years Picasso's palette was dominated by this color. Cold and deep, it was for him "the color of colors." It was ideal for expressing human solitude, misery, and suffering. Picasso was then living in difficult conditions and painted social outcasts: beggars, prostitutes, the blind. He also saw himself in blue. *Self-Portrait in Blue*, 1902.

Rose Period: 1904–1906
There are many changes in his life. He settles permanently in Paris in a studio in the Laundry Boat, an odd building given this nickname by his friend Max Jacob. He meets Fernande Olivier and falls deeply in love with her. The Laundry Boat artists often go to the circus, which delights Picasso. There he can observe the human body from every conceivable angle. In the words of the poet Apollinaire: "Acrobats seen from all sides are sculptures in space." Little by little, his palette becomes lighter. Colors become softer and more luminous. Blue gives way to rose, ocher, and faded orange. Clowns, circus performers, and acrobats become his new models, but the figure of harlequin dominates the scene.

Cubism: 1908–1915
In 1908 the word "cubism" is coined by an art critic describing Braque's paintings.

In 1907 Picasso meets Braque. Beginning in 1909, they set out together to give painting a more complete vision of reality, one that would allow it to represent the subject from every side at once. This approach was quite different from that of traditional painting, in which the subject was shown from a unique point of view.

This results in a geometric simplification of form and works that are more difficult to read.

This quest leads them to invent collage, in which wallpaper, newspaper, string, and other items are glued onto the canvas. This revolutionary gesture marked a definitive break with oil painting and destroyed the barrier between painting and sculpture.

Neoclassical Period, 1917–1924
World War I has begun. In 1915, Picasso makes a series of drawings close to the classic painter Ingres. Picasso meets Jean Cocteau and in 1917 departs for Rome to design sets and costumes for the ballet *Parade*. He visits the museums and sees a great deal of Greco-Roman sculpture. He meets Olga Kokhlova there, and in 1918 he marries her. He begins to lead a fashionable life. He paints giant figures with empty stares like marble statues. Their forms are soft and round, their colors warm. They include dancers, bathers, and mythological figures. In these years, the spirit of classicism and the antique holds sway.

Barbaric Period: 1925–1929
Around 1925, everything changes. There is an explosion of aggressive feelings, and women, his privileged subjects, begin to undergo the most violent deformations in the history of painting. These unbridled transformations take us into a world inhabited by fantastic monsters and living skeletons.

Las Meninas, Velázquez.

Studies after Las Meninas by Velázquez.
**Between 1958 and 1959, Picasso produced 40
variations on Velázquez's *Las Meninas*. In each
one, he completely reworked the light, the
placement of the figures, their gestures, and
their costumes. This one is in grisaille or
monotone.**

Boisgeloup Period: 1930–1935
Picasso buys the chateau at Boisgeloup and settles there. Marie-Thérèse Walter, whom he had
met in 1927, becomes his new model. He takes
up sculpture again and experiments with various
techniques: relief, carved wooden figures, plaster
casts, and iron assemblages.

Wartime: 1935–1945
Picasso paints a series of portraits of companion,
Dora Maar. In *Woman Crying*, she symbolizes
human suffering and the horrors of war.

Vallauris Period: 1947–1954
Picasso begins to make ceramics. A master of
recycling, he produces many assemblages using
found objects.

Dialogue with the Old Masters: 1955–1962
Picasso produces variations on works by famous
painters: Manet, Poussin, Velázquez, and Dela-
croix.

Last Works: 1962–1973
In 1963 Picasso completes 50 paintings on the
"painter and his model" theme. In 1968, he
makes the 347 drawings that constitute his *Erotic
Series*. In 1971, he executes 156 etchings with
similar themes. In 1972, he paints his final self-
portrait.

GLOSSARY

Braque, Georges (1882–1963): contemporary of Picasso who helped found the cubist movement in modern painting.

Cocteau, Jean (1889–1963): friend of Picasso and gifted French artist, author, and filmmaker.

collage: a style of art in which different kinds of material are combined on a single surface.

cubism: style of early-20th-century painting made popular by Pablo Picasso and Georges Braque in which objects are shown from several directions at once.

Gauguin, Paul (1848–1903): French painter known for his use of bright, unshaded colors and the tropical settings of many of his later paintings.

The Georges Pompidou Center, home of the Museum of Modern Art and the largest collection of cubist paintings by Braque and Picasso.

The Picasso Museum, located in the Marais district of Paris.

The windows of Picasso's studio at 7 Grand Augustins Street in Paris.

Matisse, Henri (1869–1954): French painter known for the simplicity of his designs and the innovative use of color in his paintings.

Modigliani, Amedeo (1884–1920): Parisian portrait painter of Italian origin who, along with Picasso, was one of the first European painters to express interest in primitive art.

Montmartre: neighborhood in the hilly, northern part of Paris known for its nightclubs and cabarets, the beautiful Church of the Sacred Heart, and the city's largest collection of street painters.

Robinson Crusoe: hero of Daniel Defoe's novel, *Robinson Crusoe,* who lives for many years as a shipwrecked sailor on a desert island.

Where Are the Works by Picasso?

Photographic Credits